Teen Voices
Real Teens Discuss
Real Problems™

Teens Talk About
Body Image and
Eating Disorders

Edited by Jennifer Landau

Featuring Q&As with Teen Health & Wellness's Dr. Jan

Rosen
YA™

New York

Published in 2018 by The Rosen Publishing Group, Inc.
29 East 21st Street, New York, NY 10010

Library of Congress Cataloging-in-Publication Data

Names: Landau, Jennifer, 1961– editor.
Title: Teens talk about body image and eating disorders / edited by Jennifer Landau.
Description: New York : Rosen Publishing, 2018. | Series: Teen voices : real teens discuss real problems | Audience: Grades 7–12. | Includes bibliographical references and index.
Identifiers: LCCN 2017015840 | ISBN 9781508176480 (library bound) | ISBN 9781508176565 (paperback) | ISBN 9781508176329 (6 pack)
Subjects: LCSH: Body image in adolescence—Juvenile literature. | Eating disorders in adolescence—Juvenile literature.
Classification: LCC BF724.3.B55 T44 2018 | DDC 306.4/613—dc23
LC record available at https://lccn.loc.gov/2017015840

Manufactured in China

The content in this title has been compiled from The Rosen Publishing Group's Teen Health & Wellness digital platform. Additional original content was provided by Clara MacCarald.

Contents

Introduction

Teens constantly receive messages about their appearance. Ads tell them to improve their hair, their skin, or their muscle tone. Celebrities are criticized for gaining weight—or for losing it. Internet postings make fun of how people look. Friends and family may say critical things. Is it any wonder that so many teens struggle with their body image?

Body image is the way someone sees and values their physical self. Anyone can have a healthy body image, no matter how he or she looks. But some teens become overwhelmed. Their focus on appearance keeps them from doing the things they want or need to do.

Teens with very negative body images may develop an eating disorder. An eating disorder is a mental illness in which a person develops an unhealthy, and even life-threatening, relationship with food and weight. The National Eating Disorder Association states that twenty million women and ten million men in the United States will have an eating disorder at some point during their lives.

With all the negative messages teens receive about their bodies, it can be hard to look in the mirror and value what's really there.

Common eating disorders include anorexia, bulimia, and binge eating disorder. People with anorexia have an extreme fear of gaining weight, which causes them to drop to a dangerously low body weight. People with bulimia have episodes of overeating, called binges, after which they purge. This means they get rid of the food they binged, often by vomiting or using laxatives. In

In the past, psychiatrists did not always diagnose binge eating as a specific mental disorder. Even now, some people think those that binge eat are simply lacking in willpower.

binge eating disorder people regularly have overeating episodes, but don't take action to get rid of the calories.

People with eating disorders can lose weight, gain weight, or have no weight change. Anyone can be affected. Something might trigger the illness, or it may seem to come out of nowhere. Genetics can play a role, as can other mental illnesses.

Eating disorders are dangerous. Sufferers have unhealthy relationships to food and exercising, which can damage their body or mind. They may develop other mental problems. Teens often hide their behaviors and may not even realize they have an eating disorder. The illness can cause them to resist treatment.

Fortunately, help is available. If you suspect that you or someone you know suffers from negative body image or an eating disorder, reach out. Talk to an adult you trust or seek out a school counselor or therapist.

Share Your Own Story

The stories you are about to read were submitted by your peers to the Teen Health & Wellness Personal Story Project. Sharing stories is a powerful way to connect with other people. By sharing your story, you can connect with others who are dealing with these challenges. Find more information about how to submit your own story at the end of this resource.

Depending on the severity of the eating disorder, treatment may happen at home, at a residential treatment facility, or in a hospital. Life-threatening conditions must be treated quickly. Often the next step is to interrupt unhealthy behaviors and replace them with healthy behaviors.

Along with physical healing, therapists can help a teen address the feelings and thoughts that go along with an eating disorder. Sufferers often are dealing with other mental illnesses, too. Even after recovery, a teen must be alert for relapse, which is a return of the unhealthy behaviors. Friends, family, and a treatment team can help a teen move forward.

Chapter 1

Teens Talk About Negative Body Image

Teens with negative body images have an unhealthy focus on their appearance. They're constantly critical of how they look. They might compare themselves unfavorably to people in the media or to other teens. They worry when people say things about their bodies. Even a seemingly mild comment can have a devastating impact. Body size or shape are common issues, but not the only ones. Teens can also be self-conscious about their facial features or skin markings, for example.

In 2014, *Glamour* magazine surveyed 1,000 people and found that 54 percent of the women and a third of the men were unhappy with their bodies. Most people will never look like the supposed ideal, no matter what they do. Even if they could, the negative feelings wouldn't disappear. Life is full of challenges not related to appearance. Also, teens in the habit of thinking badly about themselves have trouble stopping.

Teens may also have a distorted body image. They may be unable to see themselves objectively. And the methods that teens use to drastically change their bodies often lead to mental and physical problems.

Feeling satisfied with one's body doesn't require changing it. A teen can accentuate what she likes about her appearance and focus on accomplishments that have nothing to do with her looks.

For example, teens with negative body images may follow a rigid diet or exercise in unhealthy ways. Even if they don't develop an eating disorder, they can harm themselves.

Fortunately, any teen can learn to feel good about himself or herself, no matter how he or she looks. Friends and family can help. Some teens might benefit from working with a therapist. Teens can learn to recognize and challenge their negative thoughts. They can come to realize that all bodies are unique and can do amazing things.

Along with becoming more comfortable in their bodies, teens can appreciate other aspects of themselves. They can value their health and well-being. They can take pride in their achievements. A realistic body image frees a teen to focus on more important things.

Kenna's Story

Ever since I was in fourth grade, I have hated myself. I felt unattractive because of my weight. Being a chubby girl and wanting to fit in is hard. I always put myself down and held myself back because I didn't want to be made fun of or to embarrass myself. Over the years I tried to lose weight and dreamed of having a perfect body to show off. The months and years passed by and my body only got heavier and heavier. I fell into a dark hole of self-hatred. I wondered why I was so ugly and untalented. It wasn't until I was in seventh grade that I realized I had to change. The situation became so bad that I would decline invitations to hang out with other girls because I was so embarrassed. I would spend my time at home crying because I thought I was hideous. I decided I should spend a lot less time worrying about my weight and more time trying to build my confidence.

The changes came slowly, but surely. Sometimes I would slip when I looked into the mirror, but there were fewer days like that. I listened to songs about confidence. I cherished compliments I received instead of thinking they were lies. It also helped to compliment

A negative body image can lead to anxiety and other mental health issues, affecting a teen's ability to function effectively at school and in social situations.

other people. One night I was in my bed crying, but my mom came in and told me how wonderful I was. Today I enjoy putting on pretty clothes and makeup, even though my size has not shrunk. I take care of myself by exercising and eating healthy, because being healthy also gives me confidence.

It makes me sad to see girls go where I have gone. That deep, dark hole of self-hatred. It isn't worth it to be in there. It will only lead to things like anorexia or self-harm. You may not believe it, but you are worth it. You are beautiful. My philosophy is that everyone is pretty and everyone has at least one likable quality. Don't listen to any negativity, whether from yourself or others. Do things that make you feel happy and confident. Nobody truly cares how much you weigh. They really don't. I promise.

Alexandra's Story

I can't remember how it started, but I wouldn't be here today if it hadn't ended. Like every other teenager, I was discovering myself in middle school. I participated in soccer and even the school play, but somehow I was feeling more and more insecure about my appearance and who I was as a person. I actually was very close to getting an eating disorder. It started with skipping lunch every day and then breakfast slowly went away, too. I was so hungry by dinner time I would eat double a normal portion and then feel like I defeated the whole purpose of not eating. Then I would continue the whole process the next day. What made it worse was not even

Teens who experience disordered eating tend to feel shameful about their behaviors. They try to hide what they are doing from friends and family members.

my parents realized I was acting this way and if my friends noticed I would make up little stories about how I ate already. I always promised myself that I'd never do that, but somehow I was getting closer to an eating disorder every day.

One day after the performance of our school play a little girl approached me. I've always had a fondness for children and I dropped to one knee to talk to her. She shyly asked to see the princess, who was portrayed by one of my friends in the play. When I showed her where

Admiration from others can inspire teens to see themselves in a new light and change their lives for the better.

the princess was she simply looked at me and said, "No. You the princess." But I had just a small part as a village girl in the play.

For days I pondered what this little girl said. Was I truly a princess and not willing to accept myself for who I was? That day I began to eat a little breakfast and a little more each day until I returned to a healthy diet.

I'm proud to say that as a freshman I have fully returned to a normal diet and continue to share with students the importance of self-esteem. Teens need to know that they are truly beautiful the way they are and should accept themselves rather than giving up eating to meet some ideal. Because of my experience I've hosted an event for younger Girl Scouts that improves their self-esteem so they won't end up the way I was—struggling with almost having an eating disorder.

My advice to anyone in my situation would be to tell someone or, if you can't do that, to make a list of everything you find beautiful about yourself. I also love to write poetry and find it a great way to express my feelings.

Never stop searching for help, because as a little girl showed me, help can be offered in a million different ways.

Simren's Story

"I swear I'll start my diet tomorrow," I say to myself as I stuff potato chips into my mouth while I sit on my couch, mesmerized by these thin, beautiful actresses on my television screen. It is an endless cycle. I can say that almost everybody suffers from their own personal demons and insecurities, but I personally had no idea that mine would develop this early. When I was in sixth grade, I noticed that my body began changing compared to the other girls in my grade, particularly when I ate an abundance of food. While all my other friends could scarf down two cupcakes and three slices of pizza and still be stick-thin, I realized that I could not do that without gaining weight. The first time I experienced insecurity about my body was when I was twelve and went with my friends to the mall. I could not buy a pair of shorts because I feared that my legs looked too fat. Meanwhile, all my friends could prance around in a pair of shorts without a second thought. It all started in that moment in time. I started tearing up in the dressing room and realized that this insecurity would never escape me. Even to this day, I dread trying on shorts or jeans in dressing rooms.

I attempted to lose some weight in the eighth grade. I started off by trying to eat healthy food and walking on the treadmill for about one hour each day. But I soon got discouraged when I did not lose any weight. I became obsessed with that dreaded number on the scale. It then dawned on me that the less food you consume, the more weight you will lose. I would limit myself to about 800 calories per day and still go on the treadmill for one hour. It was obvious that I was losing weight, but my restrictions would lead me to an eventual breaking point. After about two weeks of intense restrictions on my diet and endless exercising, I would fall victim to my sweet tooth cravings and devour five cookies. After consuming that much, I thought to myself, "Well, this day is already ruined, might as well eat what I want for the rest of the day." Then, I would go for a period of time simply eating what I wanted and not exercising, which would cause me to gain all of the weight I had previously lost. It was as if no matter how hard I tried, I could not stick to my original plan of losing weight. I tried to lose weight this way all throughout eighth, ninth, and tenth grade, but my weight simply remained stagnant.

Teens are bombarded with messages to lose weight, but there's much more to life than the number on the scale.

Nobody else saw what I saw when I looked in the mirror. When I glanced at my own reflection in the mirror, I saw flabby arms, two stubby legs, and a muffin top. My body image was so distorted that if somebody told me that I was not fat, I would laugh and say, "You don't have to lie." One of the greatest contradictions of my life was that I presented myself as a confident girl who rocked her "curves" in front of society, but would escape to my room and cry about my weight at two in the morning. I would constantly ask myself, "Why did I have to be cursed with this body?" It seemed unfair to me that people were just born with fast metabolisms and had the ability to inhale food and still be skinny! Every single day I would wake up and think today is the day that I will lose weight. But I would just become even more disheartened at my current weight, which would cause me to stress eat.

It was not until the summer before eleventh grade that I discovered my love for running. I started off by running a mile in order to prepare for my field hockey pre-season, but then I realized it was a major stress reliever. Running made me feel good about myself, as if I had been drowning all this time and finally gained the courage to swim to the top. I would wake up every single day hating my body and wishing it was not mine, but finally I felt healthy and happy! Although I did not inherit my ideal body type overnight, I started running two miles a day and this truly motivated me to seek healthier food options instead of consuming copious amounts of junk food.

I do not believe that learning to love myself has been an easy journey, but I do know that hating the way I looked and restricting myself was toxic for my mind and body. I learned to love myself and embraced my beautiful imperfections in order to spread love to others in this world. The most important thing I learned was that you are blessed with one body in this lifetime and I encourage you to wake up every day and marvel at how fortunate you are to be breathing, living, and experiencing the wonders of life. The struggle I went through has taught me that a part of me will always be

Although excessive exercise can be part of an eating disorder, a moderate amount can help teens feel more at ease in their bodies.

insecure about my body, but finding something I was passionate about helped me to cope with my struggle. A distorted body image can travel with you all your life, but you have the strength to overcome this problem and realize that you are so much more than your body. Rather than focusing on the aspects that I hated about myself, I learned to admire how I had the capability to do tasks such as run two miles a day. The most beautiful things about you are the very aspects that you do not notice about yourself, but I strongly urge you to take small steps toward realizing your true potential.

MYTHS **AND** FACTS

MYTH   People with great bodies don't have body issues.

FACT   A person can feel bad about himself or herself no matter how he or she looks. While being healthy helps people feel better, the goal is to learn to accept your body as it is.

MYTH   Eating disorders are lifestyle choices.

FACT   Eating disorders are potentially life-threatening mental illnesses with complex causes. No one chooses to have one.

MYTH   If someone isn't starving to death, that person doesn't have a "real" eating disorder.

FACT   People who struggle with an eating disorder can be an average weight or overweight. It still negatively impacts his or her life.

Chapter 2

Teens Talk About Anorexia

Anorexia is more than the fear of gaining weight. It is an illness that can take over a teen's entire life. Sufferers are overwhelmed by a distorted body image. The extreme weight loss the disease causes can be deadly.

The fifth edition of *The Diagnostic and Statistical Manual of Mental Disorders (DSM-V)* reports that in any given year, 0.4 percent of young females will have anorexia. They also report that ten times as many females as males are in treatment for anorexia.

Along with restricting food, teens may exercise too intensely or for too long. They may purge after they eat. No matter what the mirror shows, a teen suffering from an eating disorder sees someone who is too fat.

Anorexia harms bodies and minds. All humans need food to function, especially teens. Starvation disrupts concentration and interferes with the systems of the body. It can cause unexpected things to happen, like a person's hair falling out or downy hairs growing all over his or her body. It can damage nerves and cause organs to fail. Anorexia can kill.

Teens with anorexia can't see themselves clearly in the mirror. The more weight they lose, the more disturbed their thinking becomes.

People with anorexia may suffer from other mental illnesses. They may self-harm, which is to hurt oneself as a way to deal with emotions, or even consider suicide. Teens who suspect someone they know is suffering from anorexia should seek help as soon as possible. Delay lets things get worse. A parent, teacher, counselor, or crisis line can connect the sufferer with professional help.

Professionals can help teens return to a healthy weight. Sufferers can learn to have a healthy relationship with food, weight, and body image. They can learn coping mechanisms, which are methods for dealing with stress and intense emotions. They can regain a normal life.

Jennifer's Story

I was always a really happy kid. You could always find me singing and dancing around. I'd laugh at anything that was even slightly funny. In 2006, when I was just nine years young, my parents separated. That really hurt me, but I still hid my sadness by trying to remain positive. It never got easier, however. In middle school, everyone's toughest time during school, girls started to judge me. I was so stressed about my parents' divorce, I started eating and was gaining weight. Girls in school would call me fat. They'd say I was weird, fat, ugly, stupid, etc. One night I really broke down when someone I thought was a good friend turned her back on me and was judging me because of my pants size. I stopped eating. I ate at most a cracker a day. My parents thought I wasn't eating dinner because I had already eaten too much earlier in the day.

When I went from 145 pounds to 120 pounds in a month, my parents started to worry. I started to look a little too thin. I was really unhealthy, and my parents and boyfriend at the time were really concerned and realized I needed help. At first I was really stubborn because I was still feeling depressed and insecure. I thought I needed to lose more weight, but really I was very underweight. One night I overdosed on Tylenol and ended up in the hospital. They took my blood three times, and I was there until five in the morning. They forced me to drink charcoal, which was warm and gross.

The time in the hospital was a real eye-opener for me, and I concluded it was time for a change. Although I was going through depression, anxiety, and insecurities, I remained strong. I went through three different therapists until I found one that I liked. The doctors put

Recovering from an eating disorder takes time. A teen may need to try different treatments and meet with a few therapists in order to find the best fit.

25

me on antidepressants. I joined a tap dancing class to meet new people and get out of the house for an hour. I found something that I liked to do. I joined my school's musical production and blocked out all those people who brought me down. It was a rough road, but I overcame my challenges and I could not be happier with where I am today.

Julia's Story

The first time I chose to starve myself, I was thirteen years old. I remember that day so vividly in my mind: entering the cafeteria beside my gaggle of talkative friends, sitting down at our table, opening my lunch bag—the sandwich, the yogurt, the grapes, the chocolate. My friends ate with little care, gossiping with their mouths open wide, spraying food when they laughed. I picked at my lunch, taking timid bites of my yogurt and letting the chocolate melt on the tip of my tongue. When the bell rang, signaling the end of the period, I'd barely made a dent in my little meal.

Over the next year-and-a-half, the voices in my head grew louder and louder, making me a victim to their merciless demands. I wasn't allowed to eat over eight hundred calories per day. I had to exercise for at least three hours a day. My grades in school dropped, my friends and family became increasingly concerned, and I fell into a dark hole of depression. I felt lost, alone, and hopeless. I considered taking my own life, though thankfully, I never had the chance to do so. Thankfully, I got help.

A teen with an eating disorder won't always reach out for help. A family member or friend may need to intervene before the illness gets much worse.

My parents sent me to an intensive-outpatient-program (IOP) called Walden Behavioral Care. Nine hours a week, for eight weeks, I was taught skills, methods, and coping mechanisms to handle my immense emotions. I put on twenty pounds and learned how to maintain my weight through a consistent diet of healthy food. By the time I was discharged from Walden's care, I no longer appeared sickly, emaciated, and miserable. My internal battles, however, were greater than ever before.

In group therapy, teens with eating disorders can support one another. A teen may feel less alone when sharing his or her recovery journey with others.

While Walden certainly taught me many useful skills, I found a new, dangerous habit to replace my starvation, as I was no longer allowed such behavior. Whenever my life became too much to bear, I'd turn to self-harm, using my own nails to carve jagged, red lines into my skin. Cutting helped me in ways that pursed-lip breathing, opposite action, DEARMAN, and emotion regulation never could. It made the pain fade; anxiety flooding from my body with each droplet of crimson blood. It made me feel free.

The road to recovery for my mental illness has been long, hard, and—at times—overwhelmingly painful. To this day, I still struggle with body dysmorphia, hence the reason my mother removed every mirror from our household. I'm grateful to have love and support, especially from my two loving mothers, to help me through each hard-fought day. Without them by my side, I don't know where I'd be—if I'd be here at all.

I'd never wish this illness on anyone else. The damage it has caused is irreversible, leaving me with scars and difficult memories that'll last a lifetime. Each day is a fight, but I have to stay positive. I have to keep plugging forward. In the years to come, I want to be a writer, a mother, an inspiration to future generations, and I'm not going to let my diseases get in the way.

Michelle's Story

Ever since I was a kindergartener, I have been known as the "Happy Girl." My tight pigtails and constant laughter brought smiles to even the most hardened faces. But that girl did not seem to exist at the beginning of my junior year. It seemed that happy girl had faded away over the past few months, replaced by someone who hid under the covers until noon with the blinds closed to shut out light.

The eight months prior had been a blur, ever since I stepped on the scale and the number eighty-eight appeared, alarming everyone but me. Words of encouragement intended to help me break my routine of eating only grilled chicken and salad seemed to fly over

Depression can lead to eating disorders, and eating disorders can lead to depression. A teen with an eating disorder may also struggle with issues such as anxiety and substance abuse.

my head. Only when the body-mass scale indicated that I had lost a significant amount of muscle did I start to see that something needed to change.

While I was recovering physically, I felt myself slipping away from who I once was. It seemed that no one could understand what I was battling. Every day became a struggle as I tried to pull myself out of bed. But something inside me told me to get up. I didn't know what it was, but there was something there, pushing me to make it through the day, promising me that tomorrow could, and would, be better. All I had to do was get up.

It's only now that I realize that small voice in the back of my mind was optimism pushing me forward. Even in my darkest hour, it could not be stifled. Even as I looked in the mirror and considered the label of eating disorder that now seemed to overpower my life, I heard something. No matter how scared I felt, optimism was my lifeboat in my sea of dread. It kept me from sinking as I considered that the world is filled with struggles. Though my struggles may not be the same as my roommate's or a complete stranger's, I began to acknowledge that each of us have our own battles and challenges. And none of us should give up.

I realized that my struggle, though unique to me, had a universal aspect to it. Any gender, regardless of label or identifiers, struggles with their identity and expectations of society. We all fear failing, though our definitions of failure vary from person to person. But when we do fall, when we do struggle, the only force that can come from within us to make us stand again is optimism. Some may call it determination, some may call it resolve, but I call it optimism. It is what drives you to the future, and this supposed failure is just a small stop on the greater road of life.

Now, when I wake up in the morning, I awake to light streaming through the windows. I know it is a new day. A new day for opportunity. A new day for me. A new day for everyone.

Ask Dr. Jan

Dear Dr. Jan,
I hate my body. People always tell me that I'm skinny, but they're just trying to be nice. I don't get why they don't understand why I'm so unhappy over the way I look.
—Brittany

Dear Brittany,
Our own view of our body is often referred to as our "body image." It's understandable that others have a different view of your body than you do. Your body image is your own internal view of how you look and not necessarily your actual appearance or how you seem to others.

The truth is many of us have a poor body image. It is influenced by culture and media, which often displays both males and females in ways that do not reflect the body shapes of the vast majority of people and leaves most of us feeling that our physical appearance is inadequate. If we have poor self-esteem or suffer from depression or anxiety, we're even more vulnerable to having a poor body image. Being overly concerned with body image can also lead to potentially dangerous eating disorders.

In order to determine if you're at the right weight for your age and height, consider speaking with your doctor. If you find yourself always thinking about your weight and how you look, consider talking about it with a trusted, knowledgeable adult or health professional.

Remember that a healthy body has more to do with good nutrition and active lifestyle than simply what you weigh. By trying to focus less on how you look and more on your other positive traits, you may begin to feel better about your whole self.

Chapter 3

Teens Talk About Bulimia

Teens who have bulimia may struggle in silence. Their bodies may appear like everyone else's, but the illness can damage their bodies and minds. With bulimia, teens binge regularly. Often the episodes are triggered by stress or by negative feelings about their body. Teens feel out of control and helpless to stop. Rather than enjoying the food they're bingeing on, they often feel numbed.

Guilt and shame come afterward. To deal with these feelings, teens with bulimia try to compensate for the binge. Often, they vomit. But they may use other methods. They may exercise too much, abuse laxatives or weight-loss medicine, or fast. They may lose or gain weight.

The *DSM-V* reports that during a given year, 1 to 1.5 percent of young females will suffer from bulimia. They also report that, like anorexia, females in treatment for bulimia outnumber males ten to one.

Bulimia is dangerous. Constant vomiting can cause problems in the digestive system. Problems in a person's mineral balance can even lead to heart attacks or strokes. Teens may be starving, which brings the same risks as does anorexia.

Professionals can help a teen disrupt the binge-purge cycle as well as help him or her recover from other coexisting mental illnesses.

People with bulimia often struggle with their body image or with other mental health issues. Feelings of disgust and anxiety can become unmanageable. The emotional distress can also lead people to self-harm or consider suicide.

Bulimia is treatable. Sufferers are using the binge-purge cycle to deal with life. With counseling, a teen can learn to replace bingeing and purging with healthy coping mechanisms. He or she can learn to understand the things that trigger binges and deal with them in other ways. This will lead to a healthier relationship with both food and life.

Jessie's Story

Perfection was all I wanted. It didn't seem like much to ask for, but in striving for the impossible, I lost myself. I was hospitalized for bulimia at the end of my freshman year of high school. Going into recovery, I thought the illness was a mistake I had made—something I had chosen to do. Now that I've been in recovery for over six months, I can see that I was wrong. The thoughts that led to my eating disorder began at a very young age and grew from there. While I was in the hospital, I wrote an autobiography concerning my eating disorder, which shows the development of the disorder.

When I was young, I always chose vegetables instead of chips and water instead of pop, and I could never be the first one done eating. I couldn't admit to anyone that some junk foods actually did taste good and I would never eat anything "bad" in front of people in order to appear to be healthy and perfect. This is how I felt I should be: perfect.

Another issue was exercise. I could never appear to be lazy. I liked to show off that I kept fit by taking part in dance, gymnastics, and various other sports—whether I had fun doing them or not. I had to be the fastest, the healthiest, the fittest, the smartest, and the list goes on. Anything less wasn't good enough to me.

It wasn't until I was nine that I started paying attention to my weight. I weighed two more pounds than

A healthy lifestyle includes physical activity, but a teen may develop an unhealthy relationship with his or her body when taking part in a demanding sport.

my best friend and she would tease me for it. It was embarrassing, shameful, disgusting, and unacceptable. I wanted to be thinner. So, every time I went to her house I insisted that we work out. I even made workout schedules for us to follow each day. We continued weighing ourselves each time we were together and each time I weighed slightly more than her I felt the same embarrassment and disappointment.

I didn't change my eating habits much that year, but by the time I was ten I decided I had to diet. I started packing a sandwich and water for lunch every day, not wanting to appear fat by eating snacks like the other kids. It also made me feel better to know that my best friend, who would tease me if I weighed a couple more pounds than her, was eating junk food while I was watching what I ate.

By the time I was twelve, we were no longer best friends. I had a new group of friends and so did she. I never felt self-conscious with my new friends. I ate whatever I wanted and they wouldn't judge me as most of them ate even more. That was my favorite year. The group that I was a part of did everything together and we always had a good time.

In the summer after sixth grade, after a year when everything seemed to be going perfectly, and the balance of my life changed. My brother had been smoking, dealing drugs, and drinking. He finally was arrested, and it destroyed my entire family. My mom turned to prayer books, my dad turned to work, and I had nowhere to turn. I couldn't tell anyone for fear of judgment. So I turned to food as a way to cope. When I was angry, I didn't eat. When I was upset, I ate everything.

By the beginning of seventh grade, I started to hate my body, or more specifically, the fat on my body. I decided that I needed to lose weight. I started with a simple diet, cutting out all fattening foods and sweets and limiting portion sizes. A few days and then a few weeks went by and I still wasn't feeling any thinner. I cut back more and more. I ended up eating so little that even after eating I felt hungry. I wasn't used to this

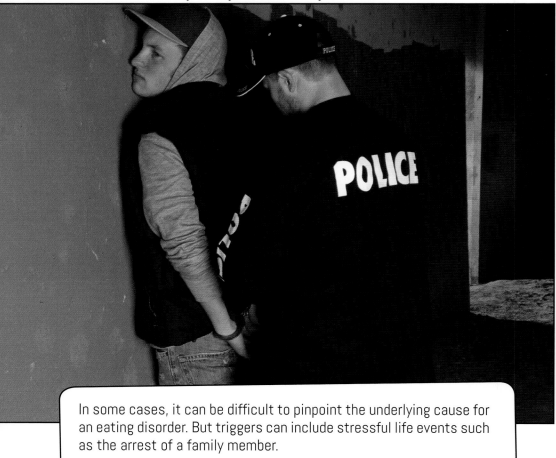

In some cases, it can be difficult to pinpoint the underlying cause for an eating disorder. But triggers can include stressful life events such as the arrest of a family member.

painful hunger. I began giving in when I got home from school. I would eat anything and everything to make the pain go away. Then I felt guilt like I had never felt before. I would exercise afterward, eat fewer calories the next day, and promise myself that I'd never let it happen again. But it always did.

I knew I had to do something about the overeating after school. I taught myself to purge. The first few times were unsuccessful, but I quickly got the hang of it and loved the feeling I had after freeing my body of the guilt from the food. This continued throughout the year. I began to get sick of the cycle: restrict, binge, purge, restrict, binge, purge. I tried to stop, but only eliminated one of the stages. My cycle became restrict, binge, restrict, and binge. I wasn't purging so I thought that meant I was better, but the thoughts were still there. I had to restrict to lose weight, and when I gave in and binged, I felt extremely guilty.

I began to gain weight and soon decided that I didn't want to live anymore if I would always be fat. At the end of the year, I attempted suicide and was hospitalized for a week.

Once I got out of the hospital, I thought things would be different. I was going to eat healthy and exercise. But still, all I could think of was food. I purged once in a while, but not nearly as often. Soon, I couldn't take it anymore. I was determined to lose weight, and purging was the only way I could make up for the bingeing when restrictions and fasting failed. So the original cycle began again. Now, I would wake up with an intention of not eating, binge by the end of the day, and purge to relieve the guilt. The cycle continued.

Even though the ending of my autobiography doesn't seem to be a happy one, it was only the end at that particular point. Now that I have been in recovery longer, I can look back and see how I fell into the trap and can prevent it from happening again. I see all the pain that I went through reaching for perfection, the impossible goal. If I ever start to slip, I can read through my past and remember why I have to stay strong in my recovery. Eating disorders are hard to overcome and even harder

Teens with bulimia often struggle with the desire to be perfect. It's not easy, but learning to live with one's imperfections can be extremely rewarding.

to understand, but there's always hope. This is coming from someone who never saw a future beyond her eating disorder and thought the only way to live was to be perfect. I'm still fighting to be E.D. free. The one thing I always have to remember is that no matter how hard I try, I can't be perfect, but that doesn't mean I can't be a good person and live a good life. It just means I'm human, which is all I need to be.

Sharon's Story

When I began bingeing and purging, I wasn't totally sure what I was hoping to gain. Perhaps it was because of an innate fear of gaining weight. Perhaps it was because of my corrosive relationship with my parents. Either way, it began as an experiment.

One day in seventh grade, after eating lunch, I decided to go to the bathroom. I was feeling a little off after receiving a poor grade on my honors geometry exam, so I decided that I needed to release my feelings. I had read books about bulimic girls purging after meals, and there was always a graphic description of how they stuck their fingers down their throats in order to trigger their gag reflexes.

As a child, I hardly ever threw up. If I did, it was always because I was either sick or had eaten rotten food. Thus, I wasn't extremely aware of what the protocol for vomiting was supposed to be. I decided that once I touched my uvula, I should have a reaction. However, after much scrabbling and scratching, nothing really happened. Suffice it to say, I was disappointed in myself and resolved to figure out how to throw up on my own time.

That night, I tried again after dinner. I had excused myself from the dinner table early, and knelt by the toilet for a full twenty minutes. Finally, after coughing for quite some time, some food came up. I didn't know how I was supposed to feel, but I did feel relieved. From then on, I made throwing up a regular occurrence. I would often purge after meals if I was stressed, tired, happy, or felt any strong emotions at all.

I didn't really feel the effects until my hair began to fall out a few months later. My mother took me to the doctor's office after a tennis match. The doctor told me that I had lost twenty pounds, weighing a measly eighty pounds. My face had grown increasingly gaunt, and I had begun to feel far more tired during the day in school, often feeling faint by the time I got home. I didn't really understand what I was doing wrong, though, and I didn't tell anyone about my purging.

Fasting or skipping meals feeds into the binge-purge cycle. A teen who struggles with bulimia may require professional help to restore healthy eating patterns.

Soon, I developed cravings for sweets and became a full-on bulimic on top of my purging. It was difficult to stop, especially since I was bingeing and purging every opportunity I had. I began to simultaneously love and hate food, seeing it both as my mortal enemy and as an old friend. As my relationships with friends and family crumbled, I drove myself further into my bulimia. I crammed food into my mouth and threw it up with as much gusto as I once laughed. In fact, I started to wonder whether I could ever laugh or smile again.

Who to Call

The following hotlines and organizations can help teens struggling with body image issues and eating disorders:

National Association of Anorexia Nervosa and Associated Disorders
630-577-1330
http://www.anad.org
10 am to 6 pm EST, Monday to Friday

National Eating Disorders Association
800-931-2237
http://www.nationaleatingdisorders.org
9 am to 5 pm EST, Monday to Friday

National Hopeline Network
800-442-HOPE
https://hopeline.com
Twenty-four hours a day, seven days a week

National Suicide Prevention Hotline
800-273-TALK
https://suicidepreventionlifeline.org
Twenty-four hours a day, seven days a week

Then came the day in tenth grade when my parents took me to see a psychologist for the first time. She asked me if I had any problems, and without warning, I began to sob. It was probably because of the unfamiliarity, but I spilled the truth out to her. Luckily, she had seen clients like myself before and assured me that there was a solution. I began to develop a diet plan and slowly I began to gain my weight back, as well as my health and happiness.

Although I still have off days, I'm more confident than ever that I am now in control of my own health. Although I do still crave sweets at times, and I still have the urge to purge whenever I get upset, with time, I know that I'll be able to return to normal.

Chapter 4

Teens Talk About Binge Eating Disorder

At one time or other, most people have felt bad after eating too much. Teens who suffer from binge eating disorder frequently experience this feeling. They eat when they're not hungry, they eat too much, they eat too quickly, or they do all these things at once. They feel out of control and helpless to stop.

The *DSM-V* reports that for a given year, 1.6 percent of adult females and 0.8 percent of adult males will suffer from binge eating disorder.

While other eating disorders can include bingeing, someone with this disorder does not regularly try to get rid of the food. The same things that trigger binges in bulimia can trigger binges for teens with binge eating disorder. Sufferers use food to cope with stress and emotions.

People are very judgmental about overeating. But binge eating disorder is a mental illness. Teens who have it often binge alone out of embarrassment. They feel awful about themselves. Feelings of shame only lead to more bingeing.

Binge eating disorder may or may not cause weight gain. Overeating and large weight gain can be hard on the body. Obesity can cause complications like diabetes and heart disease. Even without weight gain, the disorder can lead to mental health issues such as depression and anxiety.

If you think that you or someone you know is suffering from binge eating disorder, reach out. Talk to a parent, teacher, counselor, or crisis line. Binge eating

A teen who doesn't feel comfortable talking to someone in his or her life about binge eating can call a crisis line for support or for help finding treatment.

disorder is treatable. For sufferers, eating has become an unhealthy way to deal with life. Instead, teens can learn healthy coping mechanisms. They can learn to understand their triggers and how to deal with them in helpful ways. Food can return to its role as a source of nourishment and pleasure. Eating well is part of any healthy life.

Barbara's Story

When no one was looking, I would eat until my stomach ached. On some days, I would chow down half a box of cereal at one sitting. Or I would convince myself that bagels were a healthy snack and then eat five at a time. I couldn't help it and I couldn't eat enough. It was like there was a gaping hole inside me and eating helped me to fill it up.

I gained twenty-five pounds in four months. My clothes didn't fit and my weight became a major issue at home. My mom told me, "We're not going to buy more clothes for you." She blamed me for being overweight, saying I needed more self-control.

I tried, but couldn't control my eating. I often binged in secret, even though it made me feel guilty and horrible. I felt really lonely.

Then one day, my parents sat me down for a talk. Up until that point, I thought my problem with overeating would go away. But I finally admitted to my mom that I couldn't handle it on my own.

The next day, I went to an eating disorders unit at the hospital for an assessment of my eating problem.

Saying hurtful things about a teen's weight gain doesn't help change his or her behavior in a positive way. Instead, shame can trigger binges.

The doctors admitted me into their outpatient program. As part of the recovery process, I attended therapy sessions at the eating disorders unit.

At the eating disorders unit, I was forced to eat regular meals. The goal at the unit was not for me to deprive myself of food. They helped me recognize that if I ate normally, it would help me stop bingeing.

The program helped me confront painful experiences from my past as well as learn how to deal with difficult feelings in healthier ways. And I came to understand my relationship with food. Food kept me from certain kinds

Journaling is a great way to explore whatever thoughts and feelings come up while recovering from an eating disorder.

of emotional stress, but it was also a kind of protective shield. It was safety and comfort.

These days, I'm in control of my eating, but I still struggle with mini-relapses. The binges, however, have gradually become less extreme. I'm finally accepting that recovering from my eating disorder is a lifelong process. But at least now, when I struggle with it, I have the tools that I've learned for fighting the urge to eat compulsively. When I feel the urge to eat, I stop and ask myself, "Am I hungry or should I write in my journal?"

10 Great Questions
to Ask a Guidance Counselor

1. Do I spend too much time thinking about my appearance?

2. How do I recognize unhealthy messages about my body from others and the media?

3. How can I stop feeling bad about my body?

4. How can I focus on my health and wellness rather than on my body's shape and size?

5. How can I value myself for things other than my appearance?

6. Do I have a healthy relationship with food?

7. Do I have an eating disorder?

8. How can I find a professional who will help me recover from an eating disorder?

9. How can I deal with stress and intense emotions in healthy ways?

10. If I've recovered from an eating disorder, what can I do if I'm worried about a relapse?

The Teen Health & Wellness Personal Story Project

Be part of the Teen Health & Wellness Personal Story Project and share your story about successfully dealing with or overcoming a challenge. If your story is accepted for online publication, it will be posted on the Teen Health & Wellness site and featured on its homepage. You will also receive a certificate of achievement from Rosen Publishing and a $25 gift certificate to Barnes & Noble or Chapters.

Sharing stories is a powerful way to connect with other people. By sharing your story, you can connect with others who are dealing with these challenges. Visit teenhealthandwellness.com/static/personalstoryproject to read other teens' stories and to submit your own.

Scan this QR code to go to the Personal Story Project homepage.

Glossary

anorexia An eating disorder characterized by extreme weight loss and extreme fear of gaining weight.

binge An episode of eating too much food in too short a period of time.

binge eating disorder An eating disorder characterized by episodes of eating too much without trying to compensate by purging, exercising, or fasting.

body dysmorphia A mental illness in which someone can't stop thinking about perceived flaws in his or her physical appearance.

body image How someone sees and values his or her own body.

bulimia An eating disorder characterized by a binge-purge cycle.

coping mechanisms Methods for dealing with stress or other difficulties.

DEARMAN An abbreviation meant to help people deal with human interactions. It stands for: Describe, Express, Assert, Reinforce, Mindful, Appear confident, Negotiate.

distorted Being twisted, misleading, or otherwise false.

eating disorder A mental illness characterized by a disordered relationship with food and weight.

metabolism The body processe that changes food into energy.

opposite action A way to deal with unhealthy thoughts and emotions by acting the opposite to how one feels at a given time.

overdosed To have taken a dangerously large amount of a legal or illicit drug.

purge To get rid of food after eating, often by vomiting.

relapse A return to a poor state of health or unhealthy behaviors after an improvement.

self-harm The act of hurting oneself to deal with stress or intense emotions.

uvula A piece of flesh that hangs down at the back of the throat.

For More Information

Binge Eating Disorder Association
637 Emerson Place
Severna Park, MD 21146
(855) 855-2332
Website: http://bedaonline.com
Facebook: @BEDAonline
Twitter: @BEDAorg
BEDA provides outreach, education, and advocacy to
    improve awareness and treatment of binge-eating
    disorder.

The Body Positive
P.O. Box 7801
Berkeley, CA 94707
(510) 528-0101
Website: http://www.thebodypositive.org
Facebook: @thebodypositive
Twitter: @thebodypositive
The Body Positive offers professional training,
    workshops, and a youth leadership summit to help
    youth and adults overcome a negative body image.

Families Empowered and Supporting Treatment of
    Eating Disorders (FEAST)
P.O. Box 1281
Warrenton, VA 20185
(866) 662-1235

Website: http://www.feast-ed.org
Facebook: @FEASTeatingdisorders
FEAST offers educational and advocacy services for
    caregivers of eating disorder patients.

Hopewell
404 McArthur Avenue
Ottawa, ON K1K 1G8
Canada
(613) 241-3428
Website: http://www.hopewell.ca
Facebook: @HopewellOttowa
Twitter: @HopewellOttowa
Hopewell supports those dealing with eating disorders
    by providing support groups, mentoring, and a list of
    local mental health providers.

The National Association of Anorexia Nervosa and
    Associated Disorders (ANAD)
750 E. Diehl Road, Suite 127
Naperville, IL 60563
(630) 557-1333
Website: http://www.anad.org
Facebook: @ANADHelp
Twitter: @ANADSupport
ANAD helps those dealing with anxiety and fear related
    to body image and food. The organization also
    provides educational programs for families, schools,
    and communities.

National Eating Disorder Information Centre (NEDIC)
ES 7-421
200 Elizabeth Street
Toronto, ON M5G 2C4
Canada
(416) 340-4156
Helpline: (866) 633-4220
Website: http://nedic.ca
Facebook: @thenedic
Twitter: @theNEDIC
NEDIC is a Canadian organization offering education,
    outreach, and support related to eating disorders and
    unhealthy relationships around food and weight.

National Eating Disorders Association (NEDA)
165 West 46th Street, Suite 402
New York, NY 10036
(800) 931-2237
Website: http://www.nationaleatingdisorders.org
Facebook: @NationalEatingDisordersAssociation
Twitter: @NEDAstaff
NEDA supports individual and families affected by eating
    disorders and campaigns for prevention, treatment,
    and research about eating disorders.

Teen Health and Wellness
29 East 21st Street
New York, NY 10010
(877) 381-6649
Website: http://www.teenhealthandwellness.com

App: Teen Hotlines
Teen Health & Wellness provides nonjudgmental,
    straightforward, curricular, and self-help support on
    topics such as diseases, drugs and alcohol, nutrition,
    mental health, suicide and bullying, green living, and
    LGBTQ issues. Its free Teen Hotlines app provides a
    concise list of hotlines, help lines, and information
    lines on the subjects that affect teens most.

Websites

Because of the changing nature of internet links, Rosen
Publishing has developed an online list of websites
related to the subject of this book. This site is updated
regularly. Please use this link to access this list:

http://www.rosenlinks.com/TNV/Eat

For Further Reading

Ambrose, Marylou, and Veronica Deisler. *Eating Disorders: Examining Anorexia, Bulimia, and Binge Eating* (Diseases, Disorders, Symptoms). New York, NY: Enslow Publishing, 2014.

Drew, Ursula, and Stephanie Watson. *Conquering Bulimia* (Conquering Eating Disorders). New York, NY: Rosen Publishing, 2016.

Garbus, Julia. *Eating Disorders* (Issues That Concern You). Farmington Hills, MI: Greenhaven Press, 2014.

Greene, Jessica R. *Eating Disorders: The Ultimate Teen Guide* (It Happened to Me). Lanham, MD: Rowman and Littlefield Publishers, 2014.

Haerens, Margaret. *Eating Disorders* (Global Viewpoints). Farmington Hills, MI: Greenhaven Press, 2012.

Jones, Viola, and Edward Willett. *Conquering Negative Body Image* (Conquering Eating Disorders). New York, NY: Rosen Publishing, 2016.

Lew, Kristi. *I Have an Eating Disorder. Now What?* (Teen Life 411). New York, NY: Rosen Publishing, 2015.

Mallick, Nita, and Stephanie Watson. *Conquering Binge Eating* (Conquering Eating Disorders). New York, NY: Rosen Publishing, 2016.

Parys, Sabrina. *Helping a Friend with an Eating Disorder* (How Can I Help? Friends Helping Friends). New York, NY: Rosen Publishing, 2017.

Walden, Katherine, and Stephanie Watson. *Conquering Anorexia* (Conquering Eating Disorders). New York, NY: Rosen Publishing, 2016.

Bibliography

Academy for Eating Disorders. "About Eating Disorders." Retrieved February 27, 2017. http://www.aedweb.org/index.php/education/eating-disorder-information/eating-disorder-information-2.

"Alexandra's Story." Teen Health and Wellness. July 2016. http://www.teenhealthandwellness.com/article/245/10/alexandras-story.

American Psychiatric Association. *Diagnostic and Statistical Manual of Mental Disorders, Fifth Edition*. Arlington, VA: American Psychiatric Association, 2013.

"Barbara's Story," Teen Health and Wellness. July 2016. http://www.teenhealthandwellness.com/article/96/8/barbaras-story.

Cueto, Emma. "'Glamour' Magazine's Body Image Survey Has Some Disappointing News on Self Confidence." *Bustle*, October 10, 2014. https://www.bustle.com/articles/43761-glamour-magazines-body-image-survey-has-some-disappointing-news-on-self-confidence.

"Jennifer's Story." Teen Health and Wellness. June 2016. http://www.teenhealthandwellness.com/article/44/9/jennifers-story.

"Jessie's Story." Teen Health and Wellness. November 2015. http://www.teenhealthandwellness.com/article/75/8/jessies-story.

"Julia's Story." Teen Health and Wellness. June 2016. http://www.teenhealthandwellness.com/article/44/10/julias-story.

"Kenna's Story." Teen Health and Wellness. July 2016. http://www.teenhealthandwellness.com/article/245/8/kennas-story.

"Michelle's Story." Teen Health and Wellness. June 2016. http://www.teenhealthandwellness.com/article/277/9/michelles-story.

National Eating Disorders Association. "What Are Eating Disorders?" 2016. https://www.nationaleating disorders.org/learn/general-information/what-are -eating-disorders.

National Institute of Mental Health. "Eating Disorders: About More than Food." Revised 2014. https://www .nimh.nih.gov/health/publications/eating-disorders /index.shtml#pub3.

"Sharon's Story." Teen Health and Wellness. November 2015. http://www.teenhealthandwellness.com /article/75/9/sharons-story.

"Simren's Story: Body Image." Teen Health and Wellness. July 2016. http://www.teenhealthandwellness.com /article/245/12/simrens-story.

Index

About the Editor

Jennifer Landau is an author and editor who has written about psychological bullying, cybercitizenship, and drug and alcohol abuse, among other topics. She has a MA. in English from New York University and an MST in general and special education from Fordham University. Landau has taught writing to young children, teens, and seniors.

About Dr. Jan

Dr. Jan Hittelman, a licensed psychologist with over thirty years' experience working with children and families, has authored monthly columns for the *Daily Camera*, Boulder Valley School District, and online for the Rosen Publishing Group. He is the founder of the Boulder Counseling Cooperative and the director of Boulder Psychological Services.

Photo Credits

Cover TunedIn by Westend61/Shutterstock; p. 5 Preappy/Moment/Getty Images; p. 6 Zero Creatives/Cultura/Getty Images; p. 10 © iStockphoto.com/MilosJokic; p. 12 ljubaphoto/E+/Getty Images; p. 14 © iStockphoto.com/Lady-Photo; p. 15 Design Pics/Thinkstock; p. 18 © iStockphoto.com/IPGGutenbergUKLtd; p. 20 avid_creative/E+/Getty Images; p. 23 BSIP/Universal Images Group/Getty Images; p. 25 Rob Marmion/Shutterstock.com; p. 27 digitalskillet/Shutterstock.com; p. 28 asiseeit/E+/Getty Images; p. 30 imagefruit/imageBROKER/Getty Images; p. 34 Maksym Poriechkin/Shutterstock.com; p. 36 Image Source/Getty Images; p. 38 ncognet0/E+/Getty Images; p. 40 Darren Baker/Shutterstock.com; p. 42 BURGER/Canopy/Getty Images; p. 46 Christophe Lehenaff/Photononstop/Getty Images; p. 48 Peter Dazeley/Photographer's Choice/Getty Images; p. 49 Monkey Business Images/Shutterstock.com; interior pages graphic elements natt/Shutterstock.com.

Design and Layout: Nicole Duca-Russo; Photo Research: Ellina Litmanovich